Stream of Consciousness: Submerged

Derick Stephenson Jr.

First printing 2019, Kindle Direct Publishing.

Cover designed by Cody Davis. (Thanks for capturing the vision bro!)
Contact: codydavisdesign@gmail.com

ISBN-13: 978-1732604308

I'm currently Clocked: In on publishing the book. I try to tell myself that I'm doing it for multiple reasons and multiple people. It sounds good to say that I'm doing it for my mom, or my teacher who was a significant influence as I developed my interest in writing. It sounds deep to mention that I want to get my mom the house that I promised her when I was a kid. One of my goals is to be able to pay off the rest of my sister's tuition so that she can graduate. There are a lot of stories that I can concoct that makes it seem more profound.

While those things are true, I've come to the realization that I'm writing this book for me. It seems selfish at times. I'm completely fine with that. This is my self-care. This project has been the one consistent thing that I've created solely from my view of how I desire it to be. For so long, I sheltered my voice from the opinions of others, but here, I literally can tell my narrative however I choose. This has been the most liberating journey that I have experienced thus far.

Now that I'm moving into the final stages, the greatest obstacle is finishing. So much doubt seeps in. I find myself stagnant, wanting to give up. I question whether others would be interested in what I have to offer. I edit my narrative to be more appealing to others. I hesitate to invest financially out of fear that it won't be returned.

However, I'm pressing forward regardless. I'm determined to make my dream a reality.

- Major thanks to Agyeman Bonsu, CEO of Clocked: In, for the support in developing this reflection piece. Check out his page @ClockedInNow on Instagram or visit www.ClockedInNow.com for more information about the movement.

Dedications

Middle Skool D@yz A.K.A. R.I.P to the Lost Files B.K.A Repressed
Thoughts

Ms. Ratigan: Maya Angelou spoke of a woman
who threw her her first lifeline. I speak of a woman who resuscitated me

Jerry and the voices who never got to be heard

Stream of Consciousness:
"A person's thoughts and conscious reactions to events, perceived as a continuous flow."

TBC
I get stimulated. If you see tbc, recognize that sometimes thoughts be cumming too fast for me to keep up. Or, the reciprocal. If my thoughts aren't mastured, and that stimulation ain't satisfied, well… let's just say it causes more pain than pleasure.

Throwing Watches
Throwing watches into foreign territory is my method of saying that I lost track of time. Maybe time wasn't available at the time. Once I lost it, I couldn't get it back.

- Matthew White. I'm a man of my word. I'm going to get you another watch. Love you, bro.

I value writing and reflection. I want to give my readers the opportunity to document their thoughts. I am open to feedback and criticism in these sections. Feel free to use these writing pages to share your thoughts.

What are your thoughts before reading?

_____

_____

_____

_____

_____

_____

_____

_____

_____

_____

_____

_____

_____

_____

_____

_____

_____

_____

_____

_____

_____

_____

_____

_____

_____

_____

_____

I was drowning...

Thought One: Ceremonial Speech

You're definitely turning into an old man.

It's really crazy seeing how I just may be looking at a mirror image of me in about thirty years. Every time I look at your pictures, I get to see where, what seems to be, ninety percent of my physical traits stem from.

When I was a kid, I just imagined how spending every moment with you would be. Growing up with four women in the house sucked terribly. I wanted someone who I could relate to. Someone who could show me the ways of life as a man. I dreamed of how that father figure would change my life.

Though I was older when we were finally able to live in the same household, I'm glad it eventually happened. I'm glad I got to witness the man that I now aspire to be better than.

You have been such a great influence on my life. The way you unselfishly offer your time and physical effort despite whatever turmoil you may be experiencing. The way you manage your household and are so accepting of others into your home. Lord knows you have one of the most unfiltered tongues, yet you speak the most truth.

Just think, 19 years ago, I was supposed to be born on this same day. We share something more important than that. I am beyond proud to bear your name. Seeing how you have developed from being a childish, 6'1, 180 lb. boy to a 6'5, built man of God, I hope that one day I am able to fill the size 12 shoes that are placed before me.

Happy Birthday, Dad.

I know we don't say it much, but I love you man.

4.23.13, Threw Watches

Thought Two: Undisputed

Recognized for the characteristic of being particular,
Contentment only extends to settling on one thought:
The concept of reaching perfection.

Guided by the idea that greater remains,
Coerced into establishing "Greatness" as the entity's name.

Unity exhibited,
Reliance on one's brother allows the whole to stand firm.

Astray from the general,
Sharpness is key:
ONE breath. ONE mind. ONE motion.
A combination of efforts to produce ONE outcome.

Together, develops a stern posture when confronting opposition,
Maintaining the idea of inevitable triumph despite the faces who oppose.
Staying true to the qualities vowed to uphold.

Tunnel vision fixed on progress and achievement,
With rear-views attached,
Continuously moving forward,
Yet, in the same, remaining conscious of those who precede them.

It is these qualities merged,
Hearts aligned,
Actions placed to make meaning of words,
That provides for an everlasting UNDISPUTED name to be heard.

Upsilon Beta

-Bro. Stephenson Jr.

Fall '13, Threw Watches

Much love to the entire NPHC community!
06' to the brothers of Alpha Phi Alpha Fraternity, Inc.

Thought Three: Memories Fond

A risen head and immature heart
Is yet the primary for why we remain apart.
Scold me if you shall.
Deserving of it you say.
Yet, until my longing is reciprocated,
In the event that it is too late,
You'll forever be remembered as the One who got away.

7.21.14, 12:33 am

Thought Four: One Too Many

We're all the same.
Logic?
We all want to be different.
For those opposed and express that they wish to be the same
Simply reinforce the initial statement.
The irony that our differences are our
Common ground.

7.22.14, 1:48 pm

Thought Five: Fresh Air

I just want to breathe.
Sometimes I want to fly.
Sometimes I walk through that door
Just hoping I survive.
I know sometimes my Mama wonders
Is her son still alive.
Sometimes I wake up just hoping I would die.

8.8.14, 12:48 am

Thought Six: Allow Me to Introduce Myself

I was a little boy when mom and dad split.
They never married…
Guess they just couldn't manage it.
Only son, so the word of the town was I wouldn't be shit
Cause my father wasn't round.
Who would've thought?
A stupid nigga from Duval would have enough courage to prove these
Spectators wrong.
I'm far from an artist, I'm just trying to paint the picture
That I'm a king with a vision.
I'm trying to make it vivid,
With a concept of life that makes me reluctant to live it…
Why?
Some people write cause they want their stories told.
I write cause it's the only thing that heals my soul.
Like the day I found out you put your hands on my sister.
I blamed myself cause, "got damn how could I miss it!"
One time, you got mad, you caught me stealing your cologne.
If I knew then what I know now, I would've taken everything you owned.
All the way down to your life.
They blamed G for coming for you with the butcher's knife.
In reality, it was me.
I had a vision that I watched you bleed.
As you hopped in that brown Oldsmobile,
I just stood, staring, wishing looks could kill.
Tbc…

10.5.14, 11:21 am

Thought Seven: That's Love

It was nothing like that one on one encounter.
She stood there mounted.
5 feet or so. Hair not naturally gold.
I know the world is too big for my hands to hold,
But I offer it anyway.
I can't afford to let this opportunity go.
Yea yea,
Stumbling, soul fumbling,
Slight daydream about our life to come.
Before she even knew how much I'd truly give up
Just to embrace her makeup-less face
Upon the morning sun.
Focus!
Reveal your heart.
Late to my meeting to conduct this exposure.
Hands shake, lips tighten.
That spoiled bastard in my chest is pounding.
She's astounding!
With the first break of sweat,
I looked that motherfucker in the face, smiled, all 30 for showing.
And I said that's love!
First sight, I know.
I also know when I know it is…
And that right there!
"That's love!"
Chance The Rapper

10.12.14, 3:38 am

Thought Eight: Lie-On King

It's 11:50 am and I realize nothing is the same.
You and the person you once cherished most don't maintain the same
Closeness.
Friends are associates. Family members are friends.
Transitive property leaves remaining words unsaid.
Obligations appear to dominate your quality time.
Time you often spend on unobtainable outcomes.
Life, Death, Simba's story.

10.20.14, 11:50 am

Thought Nine: Alphaversary/Love You Art

"Those are some good croissants, aren't they?"

"I got a biscuit, but yes sir."

"I remember my aunt use to make the best biscuits. They would put Hardee's to shame. Of course, we don't eat them anymore because they had lard in them and that's no good for us. My aunt's four children would work from 5 am 'til the sun went down. That's all they would run off of. They did come in for lunch, but I don't know what they would eat. My cousin would get a biscuit, cut it in half, spread butter in it that sister churned the day before. He'd put it back together, poke a hole in the top, and pour fresh cream that his sister churned the day before. Those times are gone…"

Walks away

Comes Back

"My one girl cousin was the only one who continued her education. My three guy cousins went straight into World War II. Two died in the war. The other was picked up by a submarine. The sub got attacked. He made it back home but stayed in the hospital bed reading comics and watching comedies. The war changed his life. My cousin died recently. He was 89. The war changed his life. Things aren't the same anymore…"

11.7.14, 9:31 am

Thought Ten: Sunset Sails

It's 12:50.
As we lay, I look her in the eyes.
They fumble a bit.
But eventually, they lock with mine.
That's the first time I ever felt her tell the truth.
I see the autumn sky.
Slight breeze and mist.
Aging trees becoming leafless.
Tbc…

11.17.14, 12:50 am

What are your thoughts?

Thought Eleven: Mature with Age

There is nothing more beautiful than potential.
Of course, the final outcome can be a beautiful sight in itself.
Yet, what do you make of it if it turns out to be everything you never
Wanted?
On the other hand, in its levels of development,
It's everything you can imagine.
Long live the individuals who cherish the stages of growth.
If we saw what it took,
And understood where it was projected,
Maybe, just maybe,
We would be more empathetic toward the results we finally get.

11.24.14, 10:35 am

- Major shout-out to Deirdre Burton, writer and self-care advocate. Keep chasing Dee. I can't wait to see your dreams come to fruition. Follow Deirdre's inspirational posts on Instagram @deedotorg. Always love.

Thought Twelve: Cup Runneth Over

I can't watch her breakdown.
A concept that won't be understood.
But feelings wouldn't change
And every good act would be simply done in vain.
Silent as can be,
She's looking over my way.
I know in her mind she's screaming out
"Fuck You!
You saying that making love wouldn't make you fall in love too?
After all that I invested…
You weren't saying that when you were kissing on my neck.
No emotional attachment, that it was just sex…
Hell yea I'm screaming fuck you.
As bad as I want to…
This type of thinking makes me never want to trust you.
All I ever had was my pure love to offer.
But the only thing I received was the hate that I adopted.
About you, there are things I will respect,
But you'll never see through my eyes
The things you'll never get."

Just to sum up the situation…

12.1.14, 2:36 am

Thought Thirteen: Dear Mr. Clark Kent

We watching us die on our phone screens.
This once may have made a universal movement.
Now?
The idea and its application may temporarily present an uproar within the
Social media atmosphere.
That's it.
That would be the limit.
The maximum capacity.
The threshold for expression of opinion.
We would fight as long as we feel our physical identity is hidden.
For my seasoned people, that's what we refer to as "doing it for the gram."
Nothing else.
There is no longevity in our emotion.
Our historic language has been masked by euphemisms posterized on every
Screen across the nation.
The story of the underground journey is, well, just that:
Buried!
It has been desensitized.
The tracks of profound leaders have been overshadowed by "Hood" Niggas
and "Real" housewives.
The large-scale exploitation of these select idols has established intractable
Concepts that are so deeply rooted, we ourselves have begun to accept them.
It reflects.
Those who work to make these pictures less vivid are trapped
Overcompensating just to refute these perspectives.
That's why I sport this V.O.T.E.
I understand that the intelligent brother that I consider myself to be is
Publicly reduced to worthless,
Simply because of the association with this black hood.
My justification for potentially receiving a reduction on my presentation
Because of my image is
Because I understand that as long as I abide by the measures set by those
Who accept those views,
In addition to some who are to cherish me the most,
I would be continuing to conform to standards set as a generalization of who

They think I am and would like to portray me to be.
I would continue to give them,
Whoever they are,
Permission to dictate what I can and cannot do.

I'm so sorry to interrupt your scheduled program.
We have BREAKING NEWS!
THIS JUST IN!
Captain America has just disarmed the aggressive black power in self-
Defense.
Non-supporters of the triumph have been protesting ever since.
While the noble Superman has saved our lives once again.
One day I composed a letter that read:
"Dear Mr. Clark Kent,
Closed ears and an open mouth make you susceptible to lies.
That's exactly what you internal-lies.
Your eyes stay focused on the mainstream.
What you watch is what you live,
It becomes your reality.
You've seen it all before,
So much so that you can't decipher truth.
That same appeal to ignorance is reciprocated to our youth."
That's exactly why I've begun writing a letter to my unborn daughter.
I understand that one day she's going to grow up.
She's going to look at that T.V. screen,
Then she'll look me in the face with nothing but innocence and purity in her
Eyes.
She'll ask me: "Why?
Why daddy?
Why daddy don't they love us?!
How come all that we've previously been through isn't already enough?!
Daddy how long will this last?!
How long will our future continue to be dictated by our past?!"
I'll tell her:
"Well baby,
Life for you will never be a crystal stair."
I'll tell her to rest.

As my little Martin Luther Queen begins to dream
I'll sing her a lullaby:
"They look at you.
They see your pain.
They see your scars.
A blackened heart.
And yea I know,
That though it's cold,
If you look a little closer,
You'll see an ounce of old gold.
Baby go for the gold."
Then I awaken!
It was all a dream.
Word Up says that's all it would ever be.
I wouldn't know.
As I develop the Audacity of H.O.P.E. for change,
And advocate for people to believe that "Yes We Can,"
As a black man in America, the only peaceful sleep I feel I'll get is my
Eternal rest.
I just pray that by then,
The President on the screen will be courageous enough to express that
Equality will only exist upon the realization that the only race is the Human
Race.
That race should be run with endurance.

2.4.15, Threw Watches

Thought Fourteen: Black by Technicality

"Technically"
I'm an American of African descent.
But let's skip the bullshit, because
"Technically"
My parents weren't married when I was born
So by American social construct,
"Technically"
My name is Bastard.
"Technically"
I don't know the history of the bloodstream that comprises my origin.
However, I do know that I'm
"Technically"
Named after a white man, cause it's likely my last name came from my
ancestor's master.
"Technically"
I'm not racist.
I just see a lot of evil in the opposition and a lot of opposition in the white
Race.
"Technically"
It's called pro-black,
And we preach equality, when in reality we desire the black to rise while the
remainder submit to the realization of our greatness.
"Technically"
I'm not a great black man,
But a basic white man in a black body.
Because I talk "proper,"
And I don't profess that I'm a real nigga,
And I don't sell the same product that got **** addicted,
And though I've seen the rock be chopped, and grazed my hand over the
heat, I had enough sense to value life,
So I've never pulled the trigger.
"Technically"
I was Rudolph this whole time.
If I happen to walk across that stage,
They'll begin to make the Barack Hussein comparisons just to indicate that at

Least two of us made it.

"Technically"

I'm the mid filling between the sliced and toasted street slaves and the upper
Buns of corporate pimps.

With one bet for me

And two against.

Such promise for my future!

"Technically"

I'm the last of a dying breed, carrying the torch to guide a lost generation,

With a side of "I told you so," in case I fail.

Cause at that point,

Being black is a technicality, all 6'3 of me is still 3/5 of them,

And I wasn't supposed to make it this far in the first place.

2.11.15, 10:10 pm

Thought Fifteen: The Choice "To Be"

Two choices,
Enough is enough.
Either write a poem or self-destruct.
And I chose the latter.
Grab that paper and sprayed it with grey matter.
The pen transitioned to a knife.
I wrote life,
Took heed,
Took life and let my soul bleed.
And that's why you feel it…

2.17.15, 10:10 pm

Thought Sixteen: The Lineage

I can't scream fuck the white man…
I know one day in the past
~~He and my ancestor probably got their freak on~~
~~Or~~ he likely got his creep on.
And nine months later,
An offspring sprung after the rain got its leak on.
Touchy subject,
But I'm too tired of civilians acting like they're so fucking far removed
To be able to discuss it.
I know in some moment within the torture and screams
That black beauty was able to afford a sigh of relief.
Hard to conceive but just imagine.
That little nigga just got a few feet closer to the master.
Slave life after, in the house rather than
Getting ten shades blacker.
Such a fucked up view.
Probably makes me fucked up too...
But somewhere in the lost years, you'll find it was true…

2.24.15, 12:57 pm

Thought Seventeen: Role Modelz

My mom had a boyfriend.
That nigga was a misogynist.
Too young for a good girl.
More infatuated with a project chick.
The first time I ever witnessed my ma heart turn cold:
One day riding down Moncrief.
The story never gets old.
She saw him riding down the street.
Her best friend in the passenger seat.
She reached under me, grabbed the crowbar.
He hit a red light, she walked to his car.
I screamed no mama, she busted his windshield.
She felt the temporary release, but I know her heart never healed.

My mom had a boyfriend,
He said he was dedicated to the service.
In reality, the thought of commitment made him nervous.
Tbc…

4.9.15, 11:46 pm

Thought Eighteen: Made In Image

Take back the night.
The moment we put value into us,
We become valuable.
When it rains it pours.
When it rains it pours.
It rained it poured.
Then I heard an applaud.
This the type of stuff that leaves my memory scarred.
This the type of stuff that makes me envy the gods.

4.24.15, 2:14 pm

Thought Nineteen: We Played Games

When fire started,
Needed a vent.
They brought water and sand.
When fire became internal,
Needed wind to support my flames.
Recognized, the opportunity to set ablaze minds of the next legends.
Found my calling, even if temporary.
To support Kings, who by society's standards, are rendered peasants.
Cautioned
To give your heart but not sell your soul.
The unfortunate transforms both
Potential best-sellers,
As well, tongues that spoke truth,
Into verses untold.
Should one invest just an ounce too much,
They'd lose all they know and had to offer.
Wishing fire was never set.

Threw Watches

Thought Twenty: P.O.W.

I had a dream.
Of all dreams, I had a bad one.
Everything I desired was within my grasp.
Finances were a concern of the past.
Food was in bulk.
Clothes were of the latest fashion. I had the house that the eight-year-old me
promised my mama.
I had the car every street kid longed for.
That's one thing Martin Luther never told me could occur.
I guess he considered it a detail of minor status.
Because, of all dreams, I had a bad one.
Everything I desired was within my grasp.
I had watches that I threw into foreign territory.
I had shoes that cost the souls of two creatures.
I had employment that left me a servant to no man.
An appeal that appealed to anyone's interest.
I had a dream.
Of all dreams, I had a bad one.
I had everything that was thought worth having.
Except someone to share it with,
Which would've made me happy.

Threw Watches

- I refuse to say I'm self-made. Beyond that, my successes in life
wouldn't be possible without people like Jon Echols. Keep chasing
those *Coliseum Dreams* brother. Find content from Jon Echols and The
Tenth Music on Instagram @Jonechols_music and on your various
music streaming platforms.

What are your thoughts?

I was drowning…

The abrasive currents of the stream rushed mercilessly. The might of every droplet forced me beneath the surface. I couldn't breathe. Though submerged within the stream, I was conscious of the tears that flowed down. I couldn't breathe. I desperately flailed my helpless arms, hoping to rise to get at least one final breath of air. Water consumed me, filling every crevice of my lungs. I couldn't breathe.

I was drowning. It felt like there wasn't anyone there to save me…

Thought Twenty-One: Chicken Nugget Thursday

Lunchroom teacher,
I commend your effort to silence the masses.
Good effort.
Watch for the 6 in. flat top and black sweatshirt.
Watch for the half-grown women with home pressure.
3/5 men ain't no better.
Nor the Lil' miss innocence in the Christmas sweater.
Black kid across the table, I match your rhythm.
But what is your measure?
Your internal beat don't bring culture? Soul? Thirst for knowledge?
You lack drive and the wheels you roll ain't polished.
You know not what you aspire?
You know not more than one denotation of higher?

Lunchroom teacher,
Though I commend your effort to silence the masses,
Wasted effort.
Watch for the 6ft whose father's presence was abolished.
Watch for the premature mother with early home pressure.
½, part-time parents ain't no better.
Nor the big shot know-it-alls with religious spirit.
These issues are deeply rooted.
Embedded in the very DNA of each pupil's existence.

Shout on lunchroom teacher.
They hear you.
It's just their culture, soul, and knowledge are soiled in ignorance and resistance.
Though I condemn your effort,
Who am I but the 6'3, ¼ of a man who was warned to pick his battles carefully.

P.S. Save some vocals for tomorrow…

Threw Watches

Thought Twenty-Two: Note to Self

This is going to be your first-year man! It's going to be a great and challenging ride. By the end of the year, there are a few things that I want you to say you have done as an educator.

Be creative. Embrace your creative juices. Why is this important? Because you then add to the culture of the classroom. Creativity assists in meeting the needs of all students.

Be consistent. You will have good and bad days, but overall, be a fair and stable role in your students' life.

Be a part of the community. Keep investing in your community and keep letting your community pour into you.

Love you,

Derick Stephenson Jr.

8.18.16, Threw Watches

Thought Twenty-Three: Leather Jackets in July

If a soul stood amidst the blazing sun,
Conditions scorching heat,
Surely application of additional apparel
Implicates absurdity.
Yet, two souls, married to individual strife
Before they ever meet,
Join, Affix, Nest Each's Existence,
Bond their burdens, and are Christened "Complete."

What do we make of a bird imprisoned, released, recidivistic, seeking to
return to its previous conditions?

I say this of my siblings:
We found our souls within impoverished living.
Nothing brought us closer in July than that one ac unit.
That home foreclosed was our sanctuary.
Screams, blood, tears made that screened in porch our pulpit.

What do we make of a soul imprisoned, released, recidivistic, seeking to
return to its previous conditions?

Because,
It's as if we steadily lose the more we make cents,
A love I've desired to recreate that I couldn't make since.
Concluding: We may forever ask why, but some things will never make….
Like wearing leather jackets in July.

7.10.17, 5:05 pm

Thought Twenty-Four: Network

There is something beautiful about having several friends in the same general location and none of them knowing each other... Outside looking in, multiple people from different walks of life, all of which I met along my personal journey, operating in the same space, but not aware of each other's existence... that's pretty dope if you ask me... but then again, you wouldn't have to ask because I'm willingly telling you.

7.13.18, Threw Watches

- Met a beautiful soul named Bayan Founas. Her book, *Diary of a Daughter in Diaspora*, is a masterpiece. For more information, check out www.bayanfounas.com or find Bayan on Instagram @thatalgerian. Keep sharing your gifts with the world.

Thought Twenty-Five: Summer Break

Point of reflection/disappointment for me this morning: I taught over sixty-seven young minds about the caged bird, but we never discussed how to free the bird from the cage...

7.15.18, Threw Watches

Thought Twenty-Six: P.I.C.

Juxtaposition.
Life; next to you, I belong.
Batman and Robin.

8.9.17, 4:25 pm

Thought Twenty-Seven: Tired of Being Broke

At times, it can definitely feel as if the moment you take one step forward, you immediately take eleven steps backward. In the process, you stumble and fall into a bottomless pit. Meanwhile, folks begin throwing shards of glass. That is the simplest understatement of my financial status that I can offer...

9.23.17, Threw Watches

- Man! *Broken Pockets* was so real. "Middle schools need to start teaching money management." As a broke human being who is currently a middle school teacher, I felt that in my soul. Big props to Juanski. Be sure to check out *Internal Conflict* and his other work on your various streaming platforms.
Instagram: @drjuanski.

Thought Twenty-Eight: Suffer Not the Kids

Our kids need us man.

10.19.17, Threw Watches

- In my sophomore year of college, I got connected with Beautiful Kids. This organization works to support kids with Alopecia. Ms. Tieshe, thank you so much for your consistent love and support. I hope that our relationship is able to be sustained throughout the years. Find Beautiful Kids Organization (B.K.O.) on Facebook for updates on how you can support them.

Thought Twenty-Nine: The Balance

Man,

You can lose yourself in the work. I get some things are time sensitive. Then again, what is time? You're so indulged that you become unproductive. On the road to finding balance. If you have insight, feel free to message me.

10.22.17, Forgot to Set Alarm

Thought Thirty: Oppressor's Logic

Intentionally place someone in an oppressive circumstance that is meant to diminish them. Celebrate them if they are triumphant. Shame them if they falter.

That mentality is a sickness...

10.23.17, Threw Watches

What are your thoughts?

Thought Thirty-One: Roses

The sun won't rise always.
May seem farther when it's near.
You can wait until dying days.
Or you can give them roses while they're here.

10.25.17, 1:23 am

Thought Thirty-Two: Proof

"Lie to me."

11.5.17, 8:32 pm

Thought Thirty-Three: Genesis 50:20

"You intended to harm me, but God intended it for good to accomplish what is now being done, the saving of lives."

12.3.17, 11:58 pm

- Let this serve as a bet. I bet you won't make this your next tattoo. DJ Zay Crzy, I know you've experienced some challenges that were meant to cripple you, but you're still here! Keep grinding bro. Allow the world to feel your passion through your music. Keep being a man of your word. Support DJ Zay Crzy's *Man of My Word*!

Thought Thirty-Four: No Asterisk

Abundant time remedying insecurities.

Gauging the quality of society's intent, I found my success simultaneously subscripted.

Yearning, for once, to have accolades acknowledge with no

External justification for my accomplishments.

May I shatter records without the

Attachment of a star. Rather,

Note the effort and resilience that marked my place in history.

12.7.17, 12:05 am

Thought Thirty-Five: Adversary

At times, the only motivation I need is for someone to tell me what I can't achieve.

12.16.18, Threw Watches

Thot Dirty Six: 52 Pick-Up

Why you worried 'bout how many partners I've had?
All you need to know,
I'm well versed on this table.
Whether Ace high,
Joker-Joker Deuce-Deuce,
No matter what the house rule,
I'm guaranteed to win more than I lose.
Calling me out,
Tryna flip my books
Just cause I know what to do with a Maverick.
Look, I'm not your average.
You don't know the half.
I learned this game from the best.
Jack of all trades.
My dad.

Once upon a time,
Daddy said I couldn't play cause I wasn't mature enough.
Yet, my time came.
I earned my seat at the table.
Cause though mommy was more experienced, she just didn't play the same.
Daddy decided he needed a new partner,
So he showed me the game.

Lessons started out nice and slow.
Eventually, we began practicing every night.
He took his time.
No longer was I playing Go Fish.
This is Spades,
And if I were to play, I had to play right.

I learned to shuffle.
Real players bend the spine to bridge the cards.
When dealing, make them glide.
The most important thing he showed me were the private parts.
"Make sure you hide your hand.
Shhh…
Golden Rule:
Definitely no talking across the board."
"Well, what happens if I do?"

"You and daddy can't play no more."

There wasn't much else to it.
I aced every lesson.
Daddy and I ran the board together.
He was my King, I was his Queen,
As if each other's first love.
Until, one day, daddy's love became a little too much.
He would slam the cards down,
Then proceed to boast.
I wanted to quit.
He balled his fist.
"What you start you will finish."
Grabbed my wrist and forced my hand.
That filled mommy with jealousy.
He used to be her man.
Now, he'd rather play with me.

These days,
Like a deuce, wild'n in the club,
Out in public, he would joke her.
Behind closed doors, he would choke her.
When all she ever wanted was a diamond.
So she tried to
Play to win.
Went all in.
Led with hearts,
But like America, he played a Trump.
She didn't make the cut,
But ended up getting cut.
He ain't love her for what she was, but what she could create.
She decided: "I've had enough."
911, called 'em up.

That's when daddy went to jail.
It was just my luck.
Uncle took his place.
He wasn't as skilled nor was he patient.
I wanted to escape,
Flip the table,
Leave without a trace.
But I can never get away.

One day, he put the wrong card down
But forgot to pull away.
Now every time I see my son I see that Reniggas face…

These cards were never stacked in my favor.
This the hand I was dealt.
I just learned how to play it.
So you can miss me with that:
"Don't save her, she don't wanna be saved" skit,
As if I ain't tired of my heart being played with.

And ain't you here with me.
That means your hand ain't no better than mine.
Let's put this in reverse.
Show you I ain't the Uno.
I'm sure I'm not the only player in this game that you know.
Your miserable hand wants company,
And I'm the type you draw to.
I see past your poker face.
Not here to call your bluff,
Just calling a spade a spade.
What's your bid?
Are we going to go more into your insecurities or can we start the game?
It's up to you.
Make your choice and I'll follow suit.

12.28.17, 11:46 pm

Thought Thirty-Seven: New Year

Remember when the world was supposed to come to an end in 2012…

1.1.18, 12:01 am

Thought Thirty-Eight: Throwing Watches

After meeting with a group last week, I realized that one of the stories that I keep telling myself is that I am behind.

A few years ago, I created a timeline for myself that I have not been able to adhere to. I look around and I see many of my peers are engaged, graduating with their master's, or simply working in the profession that they obtained their degree in.

I kept telling myself I am behind.

Today, I had to verbally tell myself: "I'm not running a race." I'm not in competition with anyone. It is necessary to have dreams and goals. However, the value of the time that you spend on this Earth is not dictated by the rate at which you accomplish your goals. The value is in the growth and impact that you've made during the transitional period. Meanwhile, each milestone is a remembrance of how far you have come.

I have a vision of where I would like to go. I have come to terms with where I am at. Now is the time to determine what I am going to do while I am here...

The rest is for my eyez only...

1.16.18, Redundant

- I bought a shirt that read: Your Body, Your Pace, Your Results. That message, had such a huge impact on my concept of time. Much thanks to Niya Gray, CEO of Gray Expectation, for making apparel that stresses self-awareness, happiness, and identity. Check out @grayexpectation on Instagram to order your apparel.

Thought Thirty-Nine: What You Waiting For?

Ever considered that you are sitting on a talent that could transform the world?

1.17.18, Threw Watches

- I had just met you. Yet, you changed my life forever. You were the first person that I was able to sit down with and unpack what it meant to tell my own narrative. You taught me what it means to seek. *this is what it means to seek* by Yasmeen Sayyah is a must read.

Thought Forty: QTNA/Drake

If I'm confident in my hands, why would I concentrate on defeat?

1.24.18, 8:46 pm

What are your thoughts?

Thought Forty-One: F.R.I.E.N.D.S.

Part of being a real friend is knowing when you're not qualified to give advice. There are topics that I have stopped offering commentary on. I realized, on certain topics, there is toxicity in my perspective, and imposing my views on an individual who is searching for reconciliation or stability can be damaging.

If you want to continue to be a support system, work to connect that individual with another source of information outside of your personal experience.

The issue that many of us have with that is the fact that it requires us to be self-aware. We're obligated to be honest enough to admit that things we believed our entire life may be skewed.

2.4.18, Left My Watch at Home

Thought Jackie Robinson: Black by Technicality Pt. 2: Proud of My Blackness

I ain't never had to talk about my blackness.

It's not much different from some of the perspectives that I've been exposed to. I've just never had to verbalize where I <u>lie</u> on the spectrum. I've never had to openly admit that though "the colonizers" may be seen as the ultimate root of the transgressions against my identity, it was other black folk that had the most immediate impact. I ain't never tried to be white. On the other hand, I damn sure tried to be seen by my peers as black, only to be denied access to heaven. That denial sounded a little something like: "Why you dress like a white boy? Why you talk so proper? You sure you one of us?"

The contrast, in this teacher world, they easy to praise an educated black man. Most are the same who ridiculed this black man as he acquired the education. They want me to be proud of my blackness. Now I'm supposed to celebrate identifying the same as my oppressors. What happens when you're chained by the internalized self-hate of the people who you share an identity with?

2.11.18, 5:07 pm

Thought Forty-Three: Hit the Deer

The irony of the situation was that she decided to not come back home so that she could avoid driving in the night. She feared that she would not be able to see deer in the dark. Yet, in the afternoon of the following Sunday, she still managed to hit the deer.
Poor deer.
Poor, poor deer.
Mighty complex how one life can be valued more than others.
At least, that was the logic.
Three bodies inside of the car. Several cars behind and in adjacent lanes. One helpless deer.
Do you sacrifice one to save the majority? Hypothetically, you brake hard causing a large pileup. Not only do you jeopardize the life of your loved ones in your vehicle, but you also risk the death of those who trail you. Suppose you swerve, possibly into oncoming traffic or off road. Again, the magnitude of the lives impacted is heightened. The only option would be to hit the deer. It's unfortunate for the deer, but of the options, I think any human would see that as the logical decision in the mindset of humankind vs. nature. It's what brings complexity to Checkers. That sacrifice of one pawn to advance the agenda of the remainder.

Yes, my dear, you know how I can think. I'm fathoming a vision of a board of elites around a table of swine, playing Monopoly with human puppets. Pinstripes and dirty Cuban cigs. I imagine them strategically navigating through the system with some degree of carelessness. To go to jail doesn't mean the same for them as it does for dummies like me. While Jake the Jailbird's breath stalks down my spine, Mr. Elite is mighty fine while eating swine because my time won't stop his collection of rent or deals with his associates. For people like him, it ain't nothing to sacrifice one of the pawns to advance the agenda of the remainder.

For people like me, I much rather exaggerate the context of a dead deer than to bury a sister.

I'm glad you made it home safe...

2.25.18, 2:56 pm

Thought Forty-Four: Conversation About Death

"I could die tomorrow. You never know."

"Why do you have to bring up death? I hate when you talk like that."

"You hate when I tell the truth? You do realize that you are going to die one day right?"

"I know, but I don't like talking about death. It scares me."

"At one point in time, you were scared to talk to me. Now we talk every day. Applying the same logic, maybe if we talked about death more you wouldn't be so scared."

"What if I'm still scared to talk to you…"

Death Knows No Time

Thought Forty-Five: Dear Jackie

Dear Jackie,
Distance makes the heart grow fonder.
Once, you were all mine.
My only Sunshine.
I hope you understand. I had to leave.
The very thing I loved was killing me.
Distance made my soul more yonder.

Throwing Watches

- You're an inspiration because you're a success story of someone who made it out. I know a lot of people who, for whatever reason, don't get that opportunity. Now you're making waves as the Corporate Pimp. Joshua Jackson, keep growing your reach. Visit www.thecorporatepimp.com to acquire more information about how you can grow your career

Thought Forty-Six: It's Ssa

What do we invest in?
There comes a time where we must evaluate just exactly what we invest in.
What does our time, money, and energy really go toward? What do we get in
return?

I've encountered a man who is just as fed up with the apathy of our people as
I am. Yet, in true Derick fashion, to be fed up with the people is to be fed up
with myself. That's how this introspection thing works. Where am I involved
in this equation? Exactly where on this spectrum do I lie?

I've single-handedly spent someone's lifetime of funds on the food that runs
through me quicker than I ran from an ass whooping from mama. Which
doesn't necessarily convey what I intended, considering that I always got
caught. You get what I mean.
The opportunity presented itself for me to purchase the Jordan 12 "Masters."
I'm 23. What better time to cop them than while I'm on my "Master of my
fate" wave? Only to have them ruined by rain, mud, and a helplessly rotating
tire. You do the math.
The candy. The morning coffee. The clothes. The clothes. The CLOTHES.
The money that I carelessly blow. Of all of it, what do I have to show? A
crooked smile that's worse on the inside. Fluctuating weight. Another $1,000
of interest on my $40,000 (+) student loans. Other debt that I care not to
mention.
All of this to say, I dare not speak in a condescending manner toward others.
Yet, WE have been played. The kicker is we like playing. That instant
satisfaction to impress people who 1.) talk shit about us regardless and 2.) are
not much better off than us. Again, what do we have to show for it?
I witnessed this man offer $100 to his congregation for every child's future
college expenses. The catch is to have nine other supporters match $100 for
that year. That's $1,000 each year until that child goes to college. However,
that's too much of an investment. I'm not even saying that I believe in the
concept. It just seems like we're reluctant when it comes to what is truly
important. The $200 weave in the kid's hair right now is too important. The
$150 Jordans he won't be able to wear next year is too much of a priority

right now. The rims and system in the car have to be right. The clothes got to be fresh and sound foreign.

We have to turn up on Henny and Crown or else we not living right. Right? Again, for people like me, I need my golden arc friends at least three times a week to secure my spot on the dialysis V.I.P. list.

But we can't invest in the future of our kids. Oh yea, a real question followed: "What if the kid dies before they go to college?"

Well, if that's the case, chances are you'll gladly put up $10,000 to make sure the cushion in the coffin is just right so the kid's head is comfortable. Maybe even throw in a little more for the maggot repellent. So, when the church lady loses her religion in frustration, I get her. I concur. "It's ass-backward."

3.4.18, 1:37 pm

Thought Forty-Seven: Sleepless Nights

A series that is long overdue. The territory of time where I could've documented my most authentic self throughout the years. The transitional period between consciousness and death, before I'm expected to resurrect in four hours for a day's long shift of telling kids to follow their dreams. In these moments, the streams truly flow endlessly. The thoughts branch out into various directions.

I anticipate the immediate work ahead that I'm too lazy to work on at this time. I imagine my future. Wife? Kids? I said I never wanted any... What if? Moving across the country. Learn a new language in the process. What would people think of me? Kids think I abandoned them. Should've played sports in high school. Had I known I'd be 6'3... Finishing the book. What am I going to wear tomorrow? Healthcare.

I'll stop typing now…

"Time keeps slippin' away"

Thought Forty-Eight: Sleepless Nights Pt. 2: T.L.C.

Sleepless nights, up contemplating the future. On the spectrum between what I'm teaching in a few hours and my five-year plan. Somewhere along the way I question the importance of commas. I also consider working at McDonald's. This moment in particular my heart is heavy from realizing the disconnect between my family. Right about now I'm wishing I had employment that enables me to see my two nieces and nephew on their special days. I love those three little children. I want to be able to spend the day at school with them or attend their 5th 6th 7th 8th (so on) birthday parties. I consider how crazy it is that we dedicate so much of our time to other people's children yet neglect to make our flesh and blood priority. How many hugs I offer… How many weekends I spend playing ball… How many tears I've wiped away… How many words I've helped sound out… How many times I've read aloud until they've fallen asleep… None of those opportunities provided to my three little children.
I feel that guilt.
Today after I "teach" other's kids I'll be talking to Nilah through the phone. Thank God for Facetime.

HBD, Nilah...

So Late That It's Early

Thought Forty-Nine: Proud to be an American/The Right Thing to Do

"I played football… Got a little famous. I had nine scholarships. My mama told me if I was going to be a man to her, I had to marry your grandmama."

"So you married her basically because your mom said you needed to?"

"Well, I, I umm… No, because she told me it was the right thing to do. I made this girl pregnant."

FYL

Thought Fifty: Proud to be an American/Write My Wrong

"… supposed to help United States. That's me. That's me. So… I joined the service. Fucked around, met your grandmama. Fucked around, had two kids. One name was Nicey, the other one name was Janell. I couldn't support, so I joined the service. I went to the Marine Corps, cause they said they was going to protect the nation worldwide. I knew I had two motherfuckers I had to support. One name was Nicey, the other motherfucker name was Janell. But they were mine. They were mine. Forty years I hadn't seen her. Janell. That's a bitch, ain't seen your kid in forty years. Well, it was a bitch for me. For me. It was a bitch for me. Now she got kids. I ain't seen her in forty years man, it kinda ah, a bitch for me okay. I'm crying but, fuck it, these are happy tears. And ain't a damn thing none of you motherfuckers can do but beat my ass… well, you could eat me after you kill me. But fuck it… Let me see my family okay. Whether I'm right or wrong… Whether I'm right or wrong…"

Forty Years Later

What are your thoughts?

Thought Fifty-One: Proud to be an American/For My Country

"What was your mission again?"

"To kill every motherfucker that was against the United States. And I did the best I could… That's why I did it man. I got out the Marine Corps cause I started liking it. I started to like it… like this girl just took her drink okay. To me, it was good. I had to get out the service man... It was a bitch, for me. I ain't proud of it. I really, basically… Okay, when I first went, I was going for my country… After two times I got hit, damn my country, I'm going for my ass. And then, I had a wife, I had a daughter. I ain't give a thought about my country man. I had a family that was halfway, you know, try to just halfway support the best I could. Cat named Jesus blessed me man. I was ready to get a pretty good job where I could always, I always had money to take care of the family. Well, half-ass anyway. I ain't perfect, that a doggone thing. But I ain't scared to try."

Making Up 4 Lost Time

Thought Fifty-Two: Sixth Man

I didn't realize the power of substitutions until I started teaching/coaching.

One absence can significantly impact the climate of your classroom. One day of chaos and lack of structure can dampen months of routine. Substitutes for the classroom are no different than substitutes on the field/court.

Basketball has a Sixth Man of the Year for a reason. You need people who can come off the bench and at least sustain the progress that has been made thus far. It's no secret that a lot of mediocre teams may have a strong starting lineup, but a weak bench. Teams take out the players that they have been reliant on but fail to have substitutes that contribute.

We do the same thing in our relationships. Especially in that season of "sacrifice." We try to rid ourselves of things that we've been dependent on, yet, we neglect to find substitutes.

I tried to transition from pescatarian to vegetarian for a month. It wasn't sustainable because I cut a lot of things out of my diet, but I didn't substitute them with things that contributed to my end goal, which left me hungry.

There were negative people that I "cut off;" people who were draining my energy. However, I never substituted those relationships with people who encouraged me. Invested in me. Motivated me. In the end, I was left with a void.

Those were the moments where I felt lonely. The first truth was revealed. My reliance on those relationships existed only to fill a void. Failing to realize that sometimes the role players you've been dependent on just won't take you to the ship. By not freeing up space on your roster, you're not allowing the opportunity for growth and development. There will be a season when that substitute will produce more and earn the starting position.

The second truth was the revealing of my fear of termination. In short, just because people aren't cohesive with your group dynamics doesn't mean that they won't be a significant role player for another team. Yet, as long as you keep them in your system, neither team will grow.

Threw Watches

Thought Fifty-Three: Don't Shoot Da Messenger

I usually designate time to reflect.
This go around, I found myself lost and depressed.
In order to get this off my mental, I had to take a journey home.
I was surrounded by many people.
I felt alone.
Only two hours away,
But I'm feeling far from it.
Just moved to Tarboro.
Lived here for two months but I already see the injustice.
Town just flooded.
River flowing through the land like a snake, but the water is not the one
That's cold-blooded.
Dearly beloved,
Please shed your grace on my students,
Their pops, mother, sister, brother, and their cousins.
Having less is not foreign,
Losing much is more common.
What politicians spewing out is the equivalent to vomit.
Rappers only care about what's making them a profit.
Go figure!
"How Much That Dollar Cost?"
A generation lost.
You gain the world, lose your soul.
I don't need a prophet to tell me what you profit.
If these the only "icons" that are preaching like it's truth,
Tell me who gonna stick around to educate the youth.
Oh, I see…
The welfare of our future isn't a priority.
[Donald Trump] I'm sure that'll make for a great society.
Proceeds to sip tea.
But I'd be a dark hypocrite if I didn't shed light on me.
Look,
I'm down for the cause now, but I'm far from perfect.
Teaching 8th-grade language arts wasn't my original purpose.
I remember my days of Meek Mill Dream chasin'

Tryna get it all, and then some.
Until I lost it all, and then some.
I've had my fair share of being a greedy pig,
Feeding that internal bad wolf.
I was selfish.
Now I've dedicated my life to being selfless.
Caring more about the soul of the individual than their material possessions.
I don't want the fame.
You can keep the unnecessary attention.
I'm just tryna be a vessel.
And let flow through me the voices of my ancestors.
Applying knowledge that will grant power to us.
Birthing A Nation of abstract minds who spirits are rebellious.
But that would be my limit.
Planting the seed so that those who come will be provided growth and Wisdom.

Why?
Because, though I run my race with endurance, eventually the system will Catch up.
I'll be standing there with a red dot on my head proclaiming:
Hashtag,
Hands Up,
Don't Shoot
Da Messenger.

Threw Watches

- If you ever find yourself in Tarboro, NC, be sure to make your way downtowr
to Tarboro Brewing Company (TBC). Inez and Stephen Ribustello assisted me
greatly in my adjustment to the Tarboro lifestyle. Inez and Stephen, thank you so
much for your support

Thought Fifty-Four: Jordan Year

The year I was born,
Had he played in '94,
We Pippen and Jordan coming down on a fast break.
You hit a trap, but you escape.
Top of the key, I set a screen,
You go around and now you're laughing to the bank.
The crowd starts screaming your name.
To be honest, sometimes I wish it were me.
In reality, I know if I wanted to, that's a shot that I could make.
But I realize, my role lies in clearing the path for those who come,
So it's never hate.
That just goes to say,
My size 11 ½ sole purpose on this earth is to help set up the shot.
But you're the one who is designated to take it.
How dare I limited your greatness. Forgive me, Lord, for I have forsaken
The very child that you put in place to lead the next generation.
Though our paths have crossed, we have two different destinations.
Check the title.
You're a King.
I'm a messenger.
Our lifestyles have two different connotations.
This the only time I've put forth effort to be complacent.
Coming to terms with the idea that I will never witness the ripening of the
fruits of my labor.

Look...

I know you're tired of talking about slavery.
But how can these roads lead us to the future if the past didn't pave it?
If we closed our mouths and listened, the lesson we'd learn is the
Need for the individual sacrifice for the greater.
I was never one to deliver a subliminal message.
Here is me being direct.
You can have all the smarts in the world but no heart in your chest.
I'm NightJohn in the flesh.

I'm willing to take the lashes on your behalf.
I accept the challenge of being ten toes down,
Just as long as my pupils are able to walk this Earth
Exposed to notions of wisdom, perseverance, and solidarity.
When it's all said and done,
If no one else in this world lets these words flow through their teeth,
I want you to be able to say that at least you heard it from me:

You're powerful.
At no point in time should I have doubted you.
Every sentence that I speak should end by letting you know that I'm proud of you.
You have aspirations that I aspire to.
But, if you don't take away anything else.
I want you to know that true love is wealth.
Above that,
You can't love thy neighbor if you don't love thyself.

4.6.17, 4:06 pm

Thought Fifty-Five: Fire Drill

In our school, we've grown accustomed to hearing the alarm, but having a slight hesitation prior to any soul budging even just an inch. It's primarily because each alarm sounds just about the same. Infuse that with the periodic cases of false alarms and our lack of urgency for just about anything else, and you will find yourself a schoolhouse of teens walking through only one side of a double door, slowly trudging down a flight of stairs, embarking on a journey outside of what they consider prison walls, as the single tone alarm runs on like a never-ending sentence…

Then there is me. The one who just got the class settled enough to conduct a lesson on how the metamorphosis of a butterfly can be a metaphorical representation for how overcoming our fear of change can induce growth, only to be a victim of yet another inconvenient disruption. Then there was the fire drill. I instantly become the gatekeeper that encourages the wave of students to swiftly flood the stairwell, and run off into the open space, escaping the great fire that is about to consume our precious educational structure. Yet, in classic middle school fashion, the teens walk through only one side of a double door, slowly trudging down a flight of stairs, embarking on a journey outside of what they consider prison walls, as the single tone alarm runs on like a never-ending sentence… I stand there, holding the door, committed to being the last lamb that crosses the threshold of the exit on our end of the building. I stand there, amidst our hypothetically burning building, brushing the backs of every other student, motivating them to hustle just a tad bit more. I stand there, amidst our hypothetically burning building, brushing the backs of every other student, a failure in my ability to motivate them to hustle just a tad bit more. I stand there, defeated in my attempt to move them any quicker outside of our burning building than I do ushering them into our precious classroom.

At that moment, my mind is slapped with a load of questions that feel like the weight of the class set of outdated history textbooks on my back shelf. What would happen if this was a real fire? Considering no one has ever taken these matters seriously, would they nonchalantly coast through the halls of the burning building? Would everyone magically be in sync, and file through the walkways in an organized manner? Or, as the walls of Hell begin to enclose us, would all 700 plus souls scramble chaotically, shoving and trampling each other, desperately trying to be the first to report their survival of the inferno to the local news?

Rushed Out Too Fast. Forgot to Grab My Watch

Thought Fifty-Six: Black Boy Joy

Black Boy Joy.
Black Boy Joy.
There's some pain in my past that I used to ignore.
I need to bring that pain to light so I don't hurt no more.
24, still searching for that Black Boy Joy.
Black Boy Joy.
Black Boy Joy.
I'm told repetition is the father of learning,
Like being named after my father so I foster his yearning,
To be a crutch for the same people that caused him his trauma,
Labeled a boy, still got to be a man for his mama.
Black Boy Joy.
Black Boy Joy.
I started to think that's all a black boy for.
I started to think I wouldn't get an applause
If I ain't hit the stage and expose all of my flaws,
Cause where I'm from, we call that
Black Boy Joy.
Where I'm from,
In a black boy's vision is three options:
Performing, playing ball or prison.
I started to think that's all a black boy for because I noticed this difference.
Our "talk," wasn't the Birds and the Bees.
Our "talk," Survival 101:
How to manage an encounter with the police.
I guess you know what's more important,
When you ridin' on those wheels of misfortune,
The police pull you over,
The police pull you out,
The police go to Pat,
You learn not to Sajak.
I say, Jack, survive that, you better thank God.
I say, Jack, survive that, you deserve an applause.
Cause where I'm from, we call that
Black Boy Joy.
Black Boy Joy.
There was some pain in my past that I use to ignore.
But I brought that pain to light, so I don't hurt no more.
24, got a message for my young black boys.
Young black boys, I want you to know:

I'm so glad your first love was football,
But you have skills that apply to other sports that can take you global,
As opposed to a sport just being another way society puts more weight on
Your shoulders.
Got another message for my young black boys.
Young black boys, I want to see you learn magic.
I want to see the world marvel at how you make something out of nothing by
Doing a basic hat trick.
Got another message for my young black boys.
Young black boys, I want you to understand,
Hurting women that you love isn't a part of being a man.
Got another message for my young black boys.
Young black boys, I want to see you dance.
I want you to know that using your fist
Ain't the only way to allow your emotions to physically manifest.
I can send this message to my young black boys because I been there before.
Young black boys,
It only gets harder as you get older.
Young black boys,
It's okay to cry. If you ever need to, you'll always have my shoulder.
Young black boys,
Weeping may endure through the night,
But the next morning is a choice.
Young black boys, take it from somebody who has been there before.
When you're making your decision,
Black Boy, choose JOY.

Kobe Year

- As one of the few male teachers of color in my school, I recognized how important it was to connect with other peers who look like me. I couldn't help but realize just how underrepresented we are in our education system. I was glad to learn about Profound Gentlemen. Through character development, content development, and community impact, Profound Gentlemen supports students and educators across the country. For more information, visit www.profoundgentlemen.org. Keep spreading the #BlackBoyJoy fellas.

Thought Fifty-Seven: Leather Jackets in July Pt. 2

What do you make of a bird, imprisoned, released, recidivistic,
longing to return to its previous conditions?

I say this of my siblings,
We found our love in impoverished conditions.
Nothing brought us closer in July than that one ac unit.
That foreclosed house was our sanctuary.
Screams, tears, blood, made that screened in porch our pulpit.
But as of late,
We barely make time to congregate.
That's because we did just what we said.
Younger me like:
"Man, when I make it out of Jax, I ain't never looking back!"
Gone physically, but my mind still trapped.
Reminiscent of the good ol' ways,
All day, we used to play.
Tetris Attack.
Mortal Kombat on the Super Nintendo.
In between, looking out for Andre through the window.
After all these years,
Shhh…
I think I can finally hear the music.
Sounds of when the bells toll.
Every ring is like the hurts of my past mashing buttons on my control.
When I used to not care who it rang for.

Until January 28th…

I still haven't found the perfect words to say.
I know the exact thoughts I would like to convey.
The concoction of emotions to put on display.
But, I still haven't found the perfect sentence, though since you left I learned
what sin is.
It's a mental plague.
Illness of illusion.
Like how you been gone two years, but I'm still scrolling through your
Facebook page.
Check my inbox.
The guilt of the messages you sent that I never gave a response.
4 am call.

My ears pierced by the impossible.
A bullet turned your body to a dedication.
The sweetest man I ever met lying dead in the hospital.
Being 628 miles away, but still feeling responsible.
Like if I never left, I could've been there to look out for you.

It is those times of loss and grief,
That I'm nostalgic of the moments with my sisters who were always there to
Look out for me.
Cause society will do a number on you.
EVERY SINGLE DAY I have to place on my mask.
I have to put forth a front to act strong.
Meanwhile,
Around every corner,
Pain is lurkin'.
Apparitions of McClurkin.
"We fall down,"
But my sisters helped me back up.
Though we backed up,
We experienced jubilation over black songs,
And that alone gave new meaning to black women being my backbone.

So again, I ask:
What do you make of a soul, imprisoned, released, recidivistic,
longing to return to its previous conditions?
These days,
It seems we steadily lose, the more we make cents,
A love we been trying to recreate, that we couldn't make since,
Concluding: We may forever ask why, but something will never make…

Like wearing leather jackets in July.

It's like every day is January 28th

Thought Fifty-Eight: Lose My Religion

I hate black eyed peas…

But I got one of those
"If you don't like what I cooked then don't eat" type of mamas.
I try to get up from the table,
But I got one of those
"Boy if you don't sit yo…" type of mamas.
"Better be lucky I'm saved" type of mamas.
"Oh, you think you grown" type of mamas.
"Better watch your tone" type of mamas.
"I brought you into this world, I can take you out" type of mamas.
That's when I try to get smart.
"Take me out where? McDonald's?"
But I got one of those
"You got McDonald's money?" type of mamas.
"But so and so…"
"I ain't so and so's mama" type of mamas.
"Stay in a child's place" type of mamas.
"I suggest you fix your face" type of mamas.
"Quit crying before I give you something to cry about" type of mamas.

But let's not get it twisted.
I got a huggin' type of mama.
Lovin' type of mama.
Independent type of mama.
Prayer changes, olive oil, "The Holy Ghost is movin'" type of mama.
Strength of a bull type of mama.
Love so tough, when you're getting a whoopin',
You scream so loud that no one can hear your voice type of mama.
Before you get a whoopin',
She gives you a choice type of mama.
"You can get it the easy way or the hard way."
One day I chose the latter.
One day I chose to flee.
Only to glance back and see,
What looked like three generations of black women chasing after me.
Sure enough, I got caught.
I don't know what I thought.
But before she could swing, I reached up and grabbed the belt.
She hollerin', "Jesus save me from going to jail over this boy."

I'm hollerin', "Jesus I was just trying to save myself."

She said, "Boy, you gone make me lose my religion."
You should've seen the confusion on my face.
She spoke about religion as if it was tangible and could be misplaced.
She spoke about religion as if the pages in the Book of Life could be erased.
I thought to myself, "Surely this is a mistake."
But at a very young age,
I learned the hard way,
That it's best not to correct mama on what she says.
Besides,
I recognize that these days me and God ain't been seein' eye to eye.
Mama said that God would answer all of my prayers.
Lately, I been talking to the sky, but it feels like no one is there.

Reminds me of how mama will shoot me a text like, "I'm missing my son."
Three weeks will go by before she gets a response.
I know it's my fault,
But that's exactly why I hate talking to my ma.
Every time I call her,
She gets to questioning me like, "Baby what's wrong?"
I'm like, "Nothing ma."
She says, "It better be,
Unless you tellin' me that you too busy for me now so you can't pick up the phone."
I know that's a lose-lose, so I don't bother to answer.
"How you doin' ma?"
"Well son, your mama always blessed.
Just praying and havin' faith that God will deliver me from this cancer."

You see…
It's that right there that makes me feel like every conversation with God is like having a conversation with the deaf.
Because every conversation with my mama is like having a conversation with death.
Despite the severity, it's in that moment that I realize losing my mama would be like losing my heart.
If I knew it would've caused less stress, when you gave me a choice, I would've never chosen the hard.
Suddenly, I'm growing more aware of how fast the clock is ticking.
My time is being filled with regretting and reminiscing.
I'm reminiscent of us playing Tupac, *Dear Mama* on Father's Day.

I'm regretful of every time I dealt you a cold shoulder.
Reminiscent of how you showed love anyway because you said, "that's what
A mama supposed to."
I'm regretting the kisses I denied back when I was a kid,
Cause I was too afraid of showing affection in front of my friends.
I reminisce on the times I saw you interacting with the Spirit.
Regretful of the time I told you "I don't want to hear it."

But I got one of those,
"As for me and my house, we will serve the Lord" type of mamas.
"I believe God's favor will never waiver" type of mamas.
"No weapon formed against me shall prosper" type of mamas.
When the wig comes off, you know it's real type of mamas.
Hootin', hollerin' 'til she sweat type of mamas.
She hurtin', but she'll pray for her kids before she prays for herself type of
mamas.

Mama, you'd sacrifice, give us the last off your plate.
Mama, I know you were hungry for something more, I could see it on your
face.
I know you never healed when your sister got killed.
When looking for love, you found misogynists.
Fighting addiction, and its inflictions.
Every month, the doctors prescribing a new prescription.
It killed me to see my superwoman suffer physically.
I heard your cries. I heard your screams.
Thinking to myself as I walked through your door:
"What do you do when your superwoman is crippled on the floor?"

I know mama done been through things that I'll never know. She keeps it
that way intentionally.
One night, she dropped to her knees.
To the Heavens, she sent a plea:
"God cover my only son, be his screen. Shelter his eyes from all of the hurt
I've had to see."
That same night, I dropped to my knees.
To the Heavens, I sent a plea:
"God take all of my mama's pain, and place it inside of me."
Which left me with one essential question.

If we're praying for each other's pain, whose prayer does God answer?

Thought Fifty-Nine: When the Smoke Clears (2016 Reflection)

As I look back, a lot has changed. Just a year ago, 4:00 am, my family stood outside of our home, our minds scorched as we gazed at the fire that took our precious material possessions. It took a little more from me. We'll get into that later. I was excited that our minions, Diamond and Jewels, made it out safely. (Inappropriately inserts hotdog joke). In all seriousness though, I almost lost a brother that morning. See the youngin' had just made the big move from a city with a population of twenty-five to good ol' Virginia. This meant that I had to give up some of my territory. Just envision two beds with enough space to be separate, but close enough for me to slap him while he is asleep. Point of order. Fast forward to the fire. I would like to think that, despite my deep sleeping tendencies, my experiences (a story for another day) prepared me for moments like that morning. I heard the "Wake your ass up and come on" loud and clear. Someone else on the other hand still had his mouth open with his toes pointed to the ceiling. By the time that I realized I was missing a soldier, I literally had one foot out the door. Parents, if you all are reading this 1.) it's too late (No Drake) and 2.) please forgive me. Moreover, that is when it struck me: "Oh shit Daesean!" I hustled back and slapped him a few times. He woke up the first time, but I had to sneak a few more in. Following that scene, we were on our merry way outside of the burning house. I am glad that I am able to write about it so jokingly now. As a family, we were completely devastated at the moment. Individuals have received select insight into what I thought and how I felt about the situation. I took exactly one year to think about what transpired before I shared my full truth with anyone. My reflection on the healing process is what I am here to share.

One day, someone asked me about the fire. I simply said to them: "When the smoke clears, you realize that the most important thing is who you survived the fire with." I could cue the music, walk off into the distant sunset and end the movie with credits just off of that statement alone. However, I like to think of myself as a little more analytical and attention-seeking than that. So I will babble on and on about this profound enlightenment that was bestowed upon me, and create run-on sentences, and put a hidden message at the end that I will ask people about to see if they are true supporters of mine and read all the way to the end, like how I listened to all fourteen minutes and thirty-six seconds of J. Cole's Note to Self as a true fan should. Anywho! My concept of the value of life was reinforced by that tragedy. I think the picture that the higher power is trying to paint became a lot more vivid to me that day. See, I didn't stand alone that awakening morning. The news articles stated that four adults, one child and two dogs made it out of the house safely. That was more important than any object that we lost. Family became greater than possessions.

To be clear, the family isn't just nuclear. While the wings of some of our past relationships were clipped, shortening the span, new branches of our tree formed. The smoke began to fade enough for me to see who was there reaching for me in support. (Enters the shout-out zone.) **Disclaimer: Many individuals gave great effort, time, energy, and monetary support to my family during our tribulation. The support was so great, that I cannot list every individual party (Is that an oxymoron? Was that a reach? Legit questions…) If you are not externally praised, please know that you are internally cherished. Thank you! - JustDaMessenger)**

My fraternity brothers were the Phirst people that I confided in. At the time, I was their president. They helped me learn that even leaders can be vulnerable. It truly helped us grow as a unit. As a result, I was able to embody the idea that being Undisputed is not a title, it is a mindset. The next group was my Social Work class. It was at this point that I was able to tap into the empathetic energy that I was seeking. All that they offered was truly appreciated. Even the two sizes too small t-shirts. Greatly appreciated. One thing that I never spoke on publicly was the emergence of my school community in supporting my needs. I get a lot of crap from peers about my decision to go to a small school. I get ridiculed for my decision, as a black man, to attend a predominantly white institution. I acknowledge that my school has many flaws. However, there was nothing greater than President Paul Trible seeing me on the Great Lawn, hugging me, and telling me to contact him if I need anything. Nothing compared to the level of support that my University demonstrated. The very next day, I was given a check from the University's Lighthouse Fund to assist my family in getting immediate basic needs. Many individuals asked me why I lived in a sophomore "residence hall" (for my RA's out there) during my Senior year of college. That was because my University immediately worked to find me a place to live on campus so that I did not have to worry about my commute for the remainder of the year. At the time, the only available housing was in the sophomore hall, which I was completely content with. I worked in the Office of Admission for nearly three years, under one of the most encouraging ladies that I have ever encountered. I told her not to tell anyone. Yet, she shared the story with the remainder of the office. Through the concrete, my Admission family rose to the occasion to support me during my moment of hardship. Dear CNU Office of Admission, I am forever indebted to your generosity. Previously, I was definitely proud to be a Captain, but now, I know that I'm #BlessToBeACaptain.

Though that would be a happy place to halt the story, healing did not happen overnight. It was nice to have a place to stay. It was great that people offered clothing, food, and money. It was lovely how the first few weeks, people called and texted every day to check in. However, as expected, people eventually moved on, focusing on their personal priorities. As a family, we were left to manage the deeper turmoil of the situation. For at least three months, I smelled smoke and I saw fire nearly everywhere I went. It was extremely hard for me to focus in class, simply because I would envision that my professors were on fire, the board was on fire, or I would flashback to standing in the street watching the house on fire. Sleep deprivation became a real thing to me. Every single day, I woke up in a panic, sweating and sometimes hyperventilating because I dreamed about fires. Even shopping used to be hard for me. I remember shopping at H&M one day. In the store, there was a green, long sleeve button up with white polka dots. I told myself, "Hey Derick, you have that shirt." Then I remembered that I lost it in the fire. Many things people said often reminded me of the fire. It was like a class working to use a vocabulary word in the correct context. I sat in on an ASD training toward the beginning of the fall. The topic was how hard it is for students to be involved in school when they have complications at home that teachers are not aware of. The hypothetical situation that the facilitator used was a student losing their home in a fire, and just how much more of a priority that would be for that student, than being attentive in school. Just perfect. Fire even reigned prevalent in the English course that I took that semester. Several of the novels that we read maintained some reference to a fire. Let's just say, because of the title, I didn't even bother to read *Tales of Burning Love*. I struggled mentally, emotionally, spiritually, financially, and physically for an extended period of time. It felt as if I was continuously losing in every component of my life.

A turning point in my life was my internship at the Newport News Juvenile Drug Court. The staff there was amazing, understanding, and truly supportive of my well-being. Above all else, was the motivation that I got from my clients. I worked with young men who were in some pretty crummy situations. It was because of them that I regained my focus and sense of purpose. This was primarily because, once we got beyond the surface level, they began to trust me, and depend on me as a support system. At that point, I had to make a decision. I could falter and be another inconsistent figure in their life, or I could get myself together so that I could be the resource that they needed me to be. My supervisor told me, "You have to take care of yourself first before you can take care of someone else." I needed to work on bettering myself so that I could be a dependable figure in the eyes of those young men. That is an ideology that I continue to embody in the line of work that I pursue. While I was sent there to help those young men, they ended up changing my life in return. I will forever appreciate them for that.

Even what did not burn, we had to get rid of. Most people believe that when we say our house burned down, that means the entire structure was gone. While that may be true in other cases, part of the house was still standing. People didn't realize that a lot of what didn't get burned by fire, was damaged by the water from the firetruck, or the smoke. This is a topic that I would love to explore in another writing. In short, we have to learn to acknowledge every area of our life that is impacted by people and events that occur. We have to be holistic in our approach to healing. Consider what additional damage accumulated. In our relationships, for instance, we have to consider what individuals have deposited in our lives, that continuously impacts us. As an example, in a domestic violence case, physical scars may heal and not be visible any longer. However, even after an individual is removed from your life, and the visual scars are gone, what part of the structure is still standing? What additional damage do you need to remove in order to receive holistic healing, and receive a completely new building? I don't have the answers… I just felt like there was someone out there who may have needed that. Remember, I'm JustDaMessenger.

For the grand finale. What exists a year later? I'm all moved out of the house now. Of course, I get a little homesick after being here in Eastern North Carolina. I try to make great effort to see my family more. Every single time I step foot into that house, I get extremely upset that I have to take my shoes off at the door. That really bothers me. It just feels like one of those unnecessary things, that I am going to end up implementing once I get my own home. Moreover, every single time I step foot into that house, I am overwhelmed with joy. It is truly just a beautiful home. I am continuously in awe of what arose from the ashes. The hidden message is butterflies. At a young age, I fell in love with butterflies. It was really because of the caterpillar's potential. I am so glad that Kendrick released his album, which further popularized the analogy of change that occurs in a being's life. This highlights the praise shed on the final product yet acknowledges how we neglect to admire the potential of what existed before, and the process that it took to implement change. Seeing that house destroyed and rebuilt is how I began to show gratitude for the process. I can't explain why the fire happened in the first place. Yet, though I pray it never happens again, I am appreciative of the experience. Now that the smoke has cleared, I realize that so much has come from the holistic healing process.

What are your thoughts?

I was drowning...

The abrasive currents of the stream rushed mercilessly. The might of every droplet forced me beneath the surface. I couldn't breathe. Though submerged within the stream, I was conscious of the tears that flowed down. I couldn't breathe. I desperately flailed my helpless arms, hoping to rise to get at least one final breath of air. Water consumed me, filling every crevice of my lungs. I couldn't breathe.

I was drowning. It felt like there wasn't anyone there to save me...

I realized that when you're drowning, you desperately reach to grab anything that makes you feel secure. I was willing to latch on to the support of a serpent, sure that it was better than allowing my lifeless body to aimlessly drift with the ruthless flow of the stream. I was drowning. In moments like this one, I have the tendency to grasp onto anything that is offered. I reached my hand to the serpent, only to have two forceful palms clenched around my collar. In my moment of vulnerability, I reached out for support. As a result, I earned a counteracting force that thrusted me deeper into the bed of my pitiless stream of thought.

I was drowning. It felt like there wasn't anyone there to save me...

Tbc...

Photo by Malik Johnson - Instagram: @Mxjphoto2 (Love ya bro!)

About the Author

Real talk, I don't even want to do this portion. Should've asked someone else to do it. However, I want every ounce of the book to just feel personal, even though it feels weird writing a list of details about myself. I feel that most writers allow their writing to speak for them in some sense. Yet, I have a bug in my ear telling me that this is important. Here it goes...

I am Derick Stephenson Jr. I'm originally from Jacksonville, FL. That city is the burial ground for many of my darkest secrets. Simultaneously, it is a haven for some of my fondest memories. I would like to recognize William M. Raines High School for being a nurturing environment during my time there. In 2011, I transitioned to Hampton, VA. The game plan was to be in and out. Didn't quite happen as expected. I completed my senior year at Hampton High School. That is where I began to develop my writing skills. Upon graduating in 2012, I attended Christopher Newport University, majoring in social work. Throughout my time there, a significant amount of my energy was spent reflecting and writing much of what is featured in the pages prior. Present day, I live in Tarboro, NC. In this time in my life, I'm just out here tryna edumacate dem youths. Rather than continuing to babble on about me, I'd like to take the time to shout-out all my kids! Y'all are a constant motivation. Thanks for always believing in me. Thanks for trusting me to impart knowledge upon you. Love y'all.

Want to know more about me? Find me on social media: @JustDaMessenger

I learned so much from Marvel movies and Stan Lee. R.I.P

The End

You Still Here?

Introduction: Authenticity of Thought

I thought it was such a dope concept to be able to document ALL my thoughts. Everything I'm thinking transcribed to either: One of my five journals that I'll lose before the end of the year, this lengthy google doc, the notes section of my vintage iPhone 6 cellular device, the corner of a scrap sheet of paper, or the nearest paper towel that I could find. In the moments where I was most reserved, I would simply illustrate my thoughts into words that I would later add to this collection. Yeah, document ALL my thoughts. Then life knocked me upside my head with the sting of the words "***** You Thought!"

It didn't take long for me to realize the impossibility of documenting authentic thoughts. It sounds good, but what do you do when currents that once flowed fluidly like streams quickly fade into periodic droplets like after you've turned off the faucet? Or rather, the water collected from the faucet is heated or cooled beyond its original temperature. The water can be colored. Salt added. Used to boil couscous. Mixed with the variety pack of herbal tea and honey. Put into cubes.

Yea... It didn't take long for me to realize the impossibility of documenting authentic thoughts. It sounds good, but the thoughts that once flowed fluidly like streams can easily be chopped and screwed like trendy mid-2000's rap music. In a matter of moments, I've reconstructed a sentence multiple times before my pen even thinks to graze the paper. Post-conception, I still scratch the sentence out several times, chasing perfection. Derick, ain't no such thing as perfect. Will they understand it? Well, as long as you know what you mean it doesn't matter. You missed some commas. You need to write more "proper." "Ain't" ain't a word. Well, neither was fork until they created it. Should probably take the profanity out. You have a reputation to maintain... Fuck it. Just insert some thought on how language is a social construct and you'll be good. Sorry, Mama and Dada. Hope you still proud of your boy. This right here the reason why you stutter at times. Constantly filtering your words before you have the courage to allow those sounds to roll off your tongue. A coward crouching behind consciousness. So submerged in the depths of thought that you were lost. You remember when you did those three consecutive all-nighters? You started seeing things. That's when you realized that not everything is real even when you stay woke. When you gone be your real self?

Right now...

Made in the USA
Columbia, SC
08 February 2019